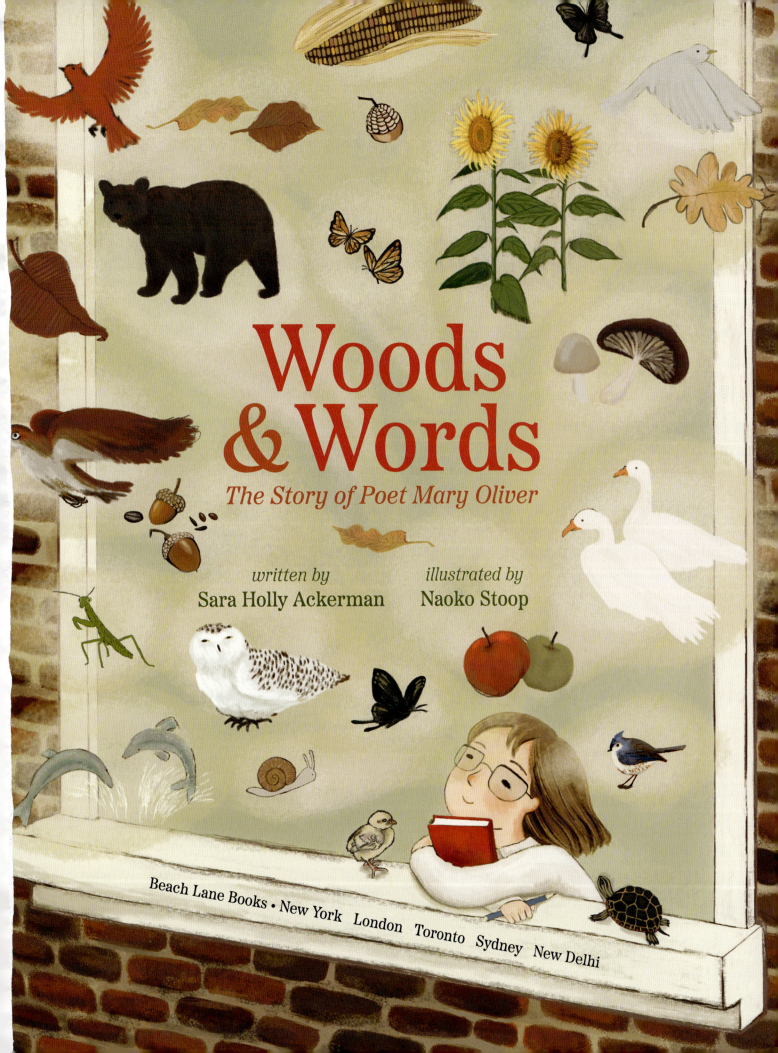

Woods & Words
The Story of Poet Mary Oliver

written by **Sara Holly Ackerman**

illustrated by **Naoko Stoop**

Beach Lane Books • New York   London   Toronto   Sydney   New Delhi

Mary crouched in the hut she had stitched of grass and sticks, noticing.
Birdsong,
velvet leaves,
a glittering beam of light.
There were treasures all around if you paid attention.

Mary traded them
for the mossy edge of a creek,
and the woods became her school.

Sitting in clusters of coltsfoot and violets,
alone except for the poets she had tucked in her knapsack,
Mary wrote.
She filled stacks of notebooks
and wore pencils down to splinters.

In spring, winged maple seeds spun off their branches, whirling through the wide, still sky.

Mary whirled off too,
zipping over pavement
and bumping along dirt roads
to an old farmhouse where a poet once lived.

She wrapped herself in woods and words.
What more could she ask for?

And then, a regular day—
just a visitor at the kitchen table—
but Mary saw it.
Love!
It took Molly longer,
but eventually she saw it too.

They captured their world,
Molly with her camera and Mary with her pencil.

Click-clack. Flash!
Scritch-scratch. Slash!

They settled in Provincetown, a speck on the map where land ended and the sea began.

Mary walked the woods searching for poems.
There were always poems if you paid attention.
She found one burrowing under
a damp,
mysterious
layer of leaves.

Mary scooped up another poem as it flashed by on the backs of two black snakes.

She smelled poems too.
Sweet or rotten, there they were.

Poems were easier to catch with the right tools:

a notebook that fit in her pocket, and pencils she kept tucked in the trees.

Mary gathered words as she walked—
along with clams in the sand flats and fat, shiny mushrooms.

For poems, yes, but also because she was hungry,
and she saw how the woods were full of supper
to bring back to the boathouse she and Molly called home.

When money was scarce,
Mary worked at a printing company.
Leftover paper scraps
were destined for the dustbin,
until she noticed they were just right
for scribbling
long,
skinny
poems.

Some of her poems appeared in magazines.
Others were bound and sold in the bookshop Molly opened.

And then, on a regular day,
with a sink full of suds and dishes to wash,
RING-RING, RING-RING.

Mary had won a poetry prize—the *biggest* poetry prize.

She nestled the telephone back in its cradle
and went to the dump.
Prize or no prize, her roof needed shingles.

But Mary thought that snow and silence,
the blinking eyes of a black bear,
and even a cob of corn were beautiful.
So she told the truth,
even if it meant a man wouldn't put her poem in a magazine.

Some people thought poetry had to be fancy,
but Mary believed poems were for everyone,
best served plain.

So she wrote what she liked,
and readers tucked her words
in their knapsacks and loved them.

When a muskrat bit her thumb,
she turned him into a poem.
The grasshopper who arrived at her plate
to lap up birthday cake frosting
became a poem too.
And year after year, her dogs
barked and bounded across the page.

That's just how Mary lived—
in a home she built
of woods and words . . .

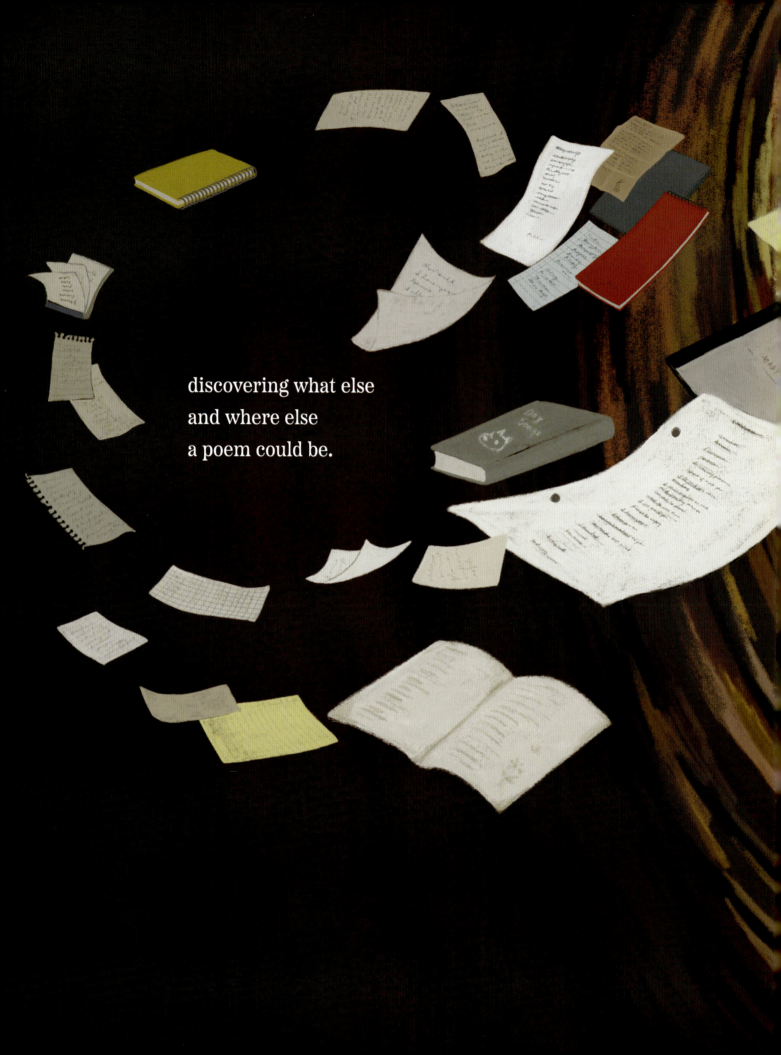

discovering what else
and where else
a poem could be.

Author's Note

MARY OLIVER (1935–2019) was born in Maple Heights, Ohio. Her home life was difficult. She sought refuge in the woods, where she would read, write, and build little houses of sticks and grass. As a teenager, she skipped class and spent most days in the woods, writing in her notebook or reading poetry books from the used bookstore, especially those by Edgar Allan Poe, William Blake, and most of all, Walt Whitman. She referred to these poets, who lived before she was born, as her friends and family. She credits her love of nature and poetry with saving her life.

Just one day after graduating high school, Mary drove to Steepletop in upstate New York, home of the late poet Edna St. Vincent Millay. She lived there, helping the poet's sister organize Edna's papers on and off, for seven years. During that time, she also attended college, published her first volume of poetry in England, and lived in Greenwich Village in New York City. At Steepletop, Mary met the love of her life, photographer Molly Malone Cook.

They moved to Provincetown, a small town on Cape Cod in Massachusetts, in the 1960s. Mary wrote and occasionally took on work that would not interfere with her poetry. Molly ran a gallery, opened a bookshop, and acted as her partner's literary agent. They lived together for forty years until Molly passed away in 2005.

Mary published her first book, *No Voyage and Other Poems*, when she was twenty-eight years old. She won the Pulitzer Prize for poetry in 1984 for *American Primitive* and the National Book Award for *New and Selected Poems* in 1992.

Despite what some critics had to say, Mary challenged the idea that poetry had to be fancy or complicated. Today, she is one of America's best-loved poets, and generations of readers have found wonder in her woods and words.

Selected Sources

Oliver, Mary. *Long Life: Essays and Other Writings*. New York: Da Capo Press, 2004.

Oliver, Mary. *Upstream: Selected Essays*. New York: Penguin Press, 2016.

Shriver, Maria. "Maria Shriver Interviews the Famously Private Poet Mary Oliver." *O, The Oprah Magazine*. March 9, 2011. www.oprah.com/entertainment/maria-shriver-interviews-poet-mary-oliver/all.

Tippett, Krista. "[Unedited] Mary Oliver with Krista Tippett." *On Being*. February 5, 2015. soundcloud.com/onbeing/unedited-mary-oliver-with-krista-tippett-jan2019.

For a complete list of sources, visit SaraHollyAckerman.com.

To the Highlights Foundation,
a haven of woods and words—S. H. A.

For Brenda Bowen,
the guiding light on my illustration journey—N. S.

BEACH LANE BOOKS • An imprint of Simon & Schuster Children's Publishing Division • 1230 Avenue of the Americas, New York, New York 10020 • Text © 2025 by Sara Holly Ackerman • Illustration © 2025 by Naoko Stoop • Book design by Lauren Rille • All rights reserved, including the right of reproduction in whole or in part in any form. • BEACH LANE BOOKS and colophon are trademarks of Simon & Schuster, LLC. • For information about special discounts for bulk purchases, please contact Simon & Schuster Special Sales at 1-866-506-1949 or business@simonandschuster.com. • The Simon & Schuster Speakers Bureau can bring authors to your live event. For more information or to book an event, contact the Simon & Schuster Speakers Bureau at 1-866-248-3049 or visit our website at www.simonspeakers.com. • The text for this book was set in Etna. • The illustrations for this book were rendered in acrylic paint, gouache, pastels, pencils, and inks and then finished digitally.
Manufactured in China
1124 SCP
First Edition
10 9 8 7 6 5 4 3 2 1
Library of Congress Cataloging-in-Publication Data
Names: Ackerman, Sara Holly, author. | Stoop, Naoko, illustrator.
Title: Woods & words : the story of poet Mary Oliver / Sara Holly Ackerman ; illustrated by Naoko Stoop.
Other titles: Woods and words
Description: First edition. | New York : Beach Lane Books, 2025. | Includes bibliographical references. | Audience: Ages 4-8 | Audience: Grades 2-3 | Summary: "A picture book biography of beloved poet Mary Oliver"— Provided by publisher.
Identifiers: LCCN 2024033526 (print) | LCCN 2024033527 (ebook) |
ISBN 9781665921855 (hardcover) |
ISBN 9781665921862 (ebook)
Subjects: LCSH: Oliver, Mary, 1935-2019—Juvenile literature. | Poets, American—20th century—Biography—Juvenile literature. |
LCGFT: Biographies. | Picture books.
Classification: LCC PS3565.L5 Z55 2025 (print) |
LCC PS3565.L5 (ebook) | DDC 811.54 [B]—dc23/eng/20240808
LC record available at https://lccn.loc.gov/2024033526
LC ebook record available at https://lccn.loc.gov/2024033527